Outdoor Adventures

By Barbara Mitchelhill

Series Literacy Consultant
Dr Ros Fisher

Pearson Education Limited
Edinburgh Gate
Harlow
Essex CM20 2JE
England

www.longman.co.uk

ISBN 0 582 84147 X

Colour reproduction by Colourscan, Singapore
Printed and bound in China by Leo Paper Products Ltd.

The Publisher's policy is to use paper manufactured from sustainable forests.

The following people from **DK** have
contributed to the development of this product:
Art Director Rachael Foster

Martin Wilson **Managing Art Editor**	**Managing Editor** Marie Greenwood
Emy Manby, Clair Watson **Design**	**Editorial** Hannah Wilson
Brenda Clynch **Picture Research**	**Production** Gordana Simakovic
Richard Czapnik, Andy Smith **Cover Design**	**DTP** David McDonald

Consultant Andy Reid

Dorling Kindersley would like to thank: Shirley Cachia and Rose Horridge in the DK Picture Library; Steve Gorton for additional photography; Dennis Lees for additional consultancy; Mile End Climbing Wall; Johnny Pau for additional cover design work; Dom Sutcliffe at Rock On for provision of clothes and equipment; and models Kwade Davis, Tommy Flay, Emily Gorton, Ayshe Khan, Rachael Matherson-Frederick, Kriyaa Mehta and Keith Watson.

Picture Credits: Action Images: Tom Hauck/Icon 32br; Alamy Images: Elmtree Images 6bl;
Buzz Pictures: Neale Haynes 4–5, 13cr; Geoff Waugh 18b, 22b; Corbis: 28b; Bohemian Nomad Picturemakers 32tr;
Pete Saloutos 36b; Phil Schermeister 4tl, 32cl, 38cl; Tom Stewart 1; Patrick Ward 17; Getty Images: Larry Dale Gordon 27;
Photodisc 3; Oxford Scientific Films: Philippe Poulet 14; Stockfile: 13tl, 33br. Cover: Oxford Scientific Films: Philippe Poulet front r.

All other images: DK Dorling Kindersley © 2004. For further information see www.dkimages.com
Dorling Kindersley Ltd., 80 Strand, London WC2R ORL

Contents

Using This Book

Outdoor sports such as hiking are great fun.

What do hiking, mountain biking and canoeing have in common? All of them offer the chance to enjoy the great outdoors while tackling an exciting sport.

Although this book gives you tips, it is good to seek expert advice from an instructor, too. It is also important always to have an adult with you.

Individual chapters on hiking, mountain biking and canoeing provide information on equipment, what to wear, planning a route, basic techniques and safety. Outdoor health and safety is explored in the final chapter in more detail. So, sit back and read. Then go outdoors and have an amazing adventure.

Guidelines for Everyone

Follow the rules below and on the next page to stay safe – and protect the environment.

Before the Trip

- Leave information in writing about where you are going and when you plan to be back.
- Check the weather forecast and dress appropriately. Remember that bright clothes make you easier to find if you get lost.
- Check that any equipment you are taking is in good working order.
- Check that your first-aid kit is complete and that you know how to use it (see page 39).
- Pack a bag to bring back your rubbish.

Take a waterproof jacket in case it rains.

During the Trip

- Stay with your group and follow the leader's instructions.

- If you become lost, then stay where you are, unless you can easily retrace your steps.

- At the first sign of bad weather, look for shelter.

- Do not disturb the wildlife. This is dangerous both for you and for the animals.

- Do not disturb plants, and never eat them. Remember that many plants are poisonous.

- Don't pollute the countryside. Take any clothing, equipment and rubbish back home with you.

- Remember that noise pollutes, too. Don't disturb other people or wildlife by shouting.

Outdoor adventures require teamwork. Make decisions together and help each other.

Always shut gates unless otherwise indicated. Walk around the edges of fields, not across them.

Never pick flowers or pull up plants. This damages the environment.

Hiking

Hiking gives you the chance to appreciate forests, rivers and mountains. It is a fairly simple activity, and you don't need much equipment. All you need is a pair of sturdy walking shoes, a map and a small rucksack to carry a few important items.

Getting Ready

Take the proper equipment and clothing when you go hiking. Some things are essential for all hiking trips, but other items aren't. Think carefully about what to take and remember that if you pack too much, it will be difficult to carry.

A map should have footpaths and landmarks clearly marked.

Equipment

Even if it is a cold day, take plenty of water to keep yourself hydrated. Always carry food to keep your energy levels up, and bring a first-aid kit. If it is sunny you will need insect repellent, suncream and sunglasses. Pages 37 to 39 give you more health and first-aid tips for outdoor sports.

Take a map, a compass and a watch. The map should show all the footpaths you will be using clearly. Other items, such as binoculars and a camera, are useful, though not essential.

A compass can help you to navigate.

A wristwatch can help you go home on time and before the Sun sets.

A mobile phone is useful to call for help in an emergency. Keep the phone in a protective case.

Safety pins are useful for torn rucksacks or clothing.

A whistle is useful for signalling for help in a remote area.

Take a torch and spare batteries in case it gets dark sooner than expected.

Choose an insect repellent that will protect you all day.

Apply suncream before going outdoors.

Take more water than you think you'll need, and make sure you drink it.

Take food and eat small amounts frequently to keep up your energy levels.

Sunglasses protect your eyes from harmful rays.

A first-aid kit is essential (see page 39).

padded shoulder straps

side pocket

webbing for attaching clothes

Hints and Tips

Pack heavy items at the top of your rucksack. Keep them, close to your back to make the weight easier to carry. Put your clothes inside plastic bags to keep them dry just in case your rucksack gets wet.

Clothing

Wear lots of layers of outdoor clothing. Then you can add more layers or take off layers as necessary. Layers of clothes trap air between them which keeps you warm when it's cold. When it's hot, remember that light-coloured clothes reflect heat and keep you cool. Pockets are useful for storing small items.

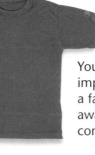

Your bottom layer is the most important. Wear a top made of a fabric that draws moisture away from you to keep you comfortable and dry.

Loose-fitting trousers let you move about freely. Trouser legs that zip off to make shorts are perfect if you start to feel hot during your hike.

The middle layer of your hiking gear should provide insulation. A jumper or fleece jacket works well.

Take a waterproof jacket as an outer layer. This will protect you from wind and rain.

Don't forget to protect your head when you pack your hiking clothes. A hat is a hiker's friend in both warm and cold weather. In winter, you lose about one third of your body heat through your head and hands. A warm hat and gloves will help to conserve heat. Wear a hat in warm weather, too. It provides shade from the Sun and protection from ticks, which can be a problem on woodland hikes.

A warm hat helps to conserve your body heat.

In hot weather, a hat protects you from the Sun and from insects.

In cold weather, wear gloves that cover your wrists. Attach them to your clothing with a cord so you don't lose them.

Thick socks protect your feet from blisters. Wear socks with padded heels and toes for extra comfort. Take a spare pair in case the socks you are wearing get wet.

Hints and Tips

Hiking in a new pair of walking boots will give you blisters. To avoid this, wear them in at home first before hiking in them.

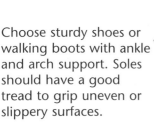

Choose sturdy shoes or walking boots with ankle and arch support. Soles should have a good tread to grip uneven or slippery surfaces.

→ Step Two:
Choosing a Route

When choosing a route find one that everyone will enjoy. There are three main factors to consider: length, degree of roughness and steepness. A map of the route will show you these things.

Public parks often provide hiking maps. Some maps may be found in your local library or on the internet. However, you may not need a map for all hikes, as many parks have clearly marked signposts for you to follow.

How to Read a Map for Hiking

Map symbols represent landmarks such as footpaths, roads and rivers. Every map has a key that explains what each symbol represents.

1 Look at the landmarks around you and find them on your map, using the key.

2 Turn the map so that the landmarks on the map line up with the landmarks that you can see around you.

3 Use the map scale to estimate how far it is to your destination.

4 Look at the map's contour lines to determine how steep the route is. (See page 14 for more about contour lines.)

5 Plan rest stops based on the distances and steepness of the route.

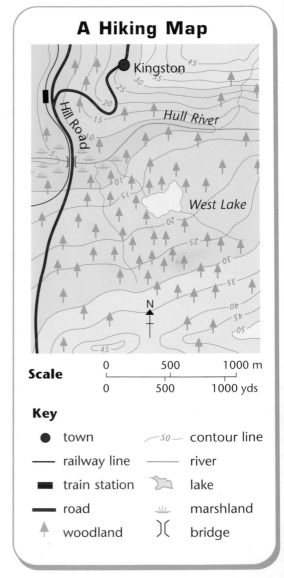

A Hiking Map

Kingston

Hill Road

Hull River

West Lake

N

Scale

| 0 | 500 | 1000 m |
| 0 | 500 | 1000 yds |

Key

● town   ‿50‿ contour line

— railway line   —— river

■ train station   ⬡ lake

— road   )(bridge

♠ woodland

12

Length

Consider how far the group would like to hike. Most people can stroll 1.5 kilometres along level ground in about twenty minutes. Include time to rest when estimating how long a route will take to walk. Ten minutes of rest for every hour of walking is reasonable. Route distances should be marked in guidebooks, on maps and by signposts along the way.

Roughness

Surfaces range from smooth and wide to narrow, rugged and rocky. Start with a flat route first. Then you will be able to concentrate more on the sights and sounds around you, without worrying about stumbling over rocks and other obstacles. A route's roughness is usually described in the guidebook

Keep checking your map to find out what the route is like ahead.

Hints and Tips

If your route is hard to follow, then refer to your map frequently. Stop every few minutes to check your location. This will help you stay in the right direction. Bear in mind that it is easy to lose your way through woodland areas.

Steepness

A guidebook or a map will warn you of steep inclines, or hills, on a route. Contour lines on a map show you how steep an area is. These lines link all the points on the map that are of equal height. A footpath that crosses contour lines that are close together is steep. As you plan your hike, bear in mind that every contour line you cross, going up or down, will add about one minute to your journey.

When tackling a steep uphill or downhill slope, slow down. When walking down a hill, place your feet farther apart for extra balance and lean backwards slightly. When walking uphill, take smaller steps and lean forwards slightly.

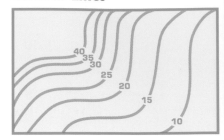

Each contour line marks a different level of elevation, indicated by a number that represents height above sea level. The closer the contour lines, the steeper the incline. Use the numbers to work out whether the incline is going up or down.

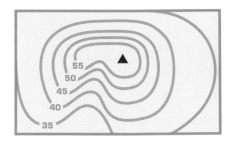

A hill is indicated by a series of circular contour lines. The peak of a hill is sometimes marked with a solid triangle or an X.

Hints and Tips

The "rest step" helps you climb very steep hills without getting completely out of breath. Step forward and put your foot down. Pause, keeping your weight on your back foot. Next, shift your weight to your front foot and take a step forward. Pause again.

Step Three:
Trying Out the Basics

When you go hiking, you need to know where you are and where you are going. Always stay on marked footpaths. Pay attention to your surroundings. Look out for landmarks to help you keep track of where you are. A compass is useful if you know how to use it.

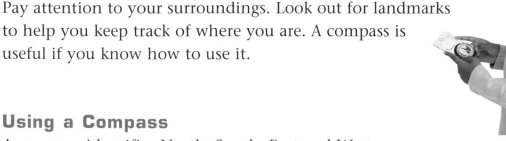

Using a Compass

A compass identifies North, South, East and West so you can work out where you are. A compass needle always points towards magnetic North.

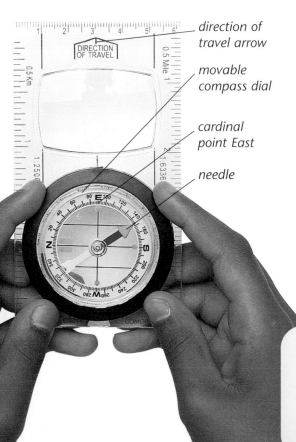

direction of travel arrow

movable compass dial

cardinal point East

needle

1 Take a good look at your compass and identify the direction of travel arrow, the movable compass dial (also called the compass housing), the needle and the cardinal points – North (N), South (S), East (E) and West (W).

2 Turn the compass dial so that the cardinal direction that you want to take points towards the direction of travel arrow.

3 Turn your body around slowly until the needle points towards north on the compass dial. Now walk in the direction shown by the direction of travel arrow.

Hints and Tips

If your compass doesn't have a movable dial or a direction of travel arrow, then turn your body until the needle aligns with N. You are now facing North.

Using Your Watch to Navigate

If you don't have a compass or if it breaks, then use your watch face to find out where North and South are. If you are wearing a digital watch, then try to imagine what it would look like with clock hands, or draw a clock face on the ground with a stick. Set your watch to the true local time (do not adjust for daylight saving time).

Hints and Tips

As you walk along, look behind you every so often. If you end up returning along the same trail, then you'll find it useful to know what the route looks like from the opposite direction.

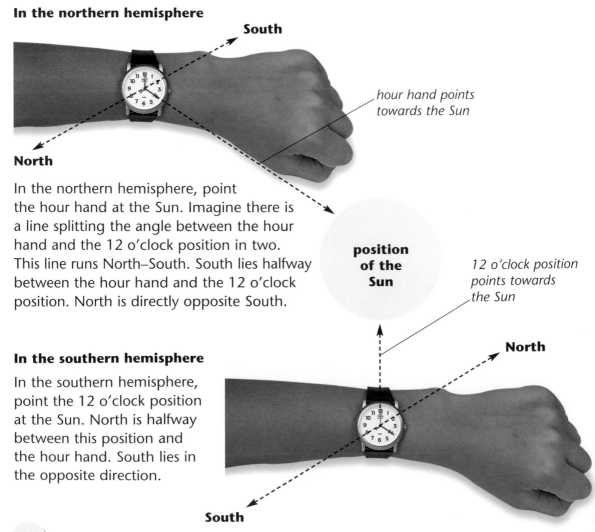

In the northern hemisphere

South

hour hand points towards the Sun

North

In the northern hemisphere, point the hour hand at the Sun. Imagine there is a line splitting the angle between the hour hand and the 12 o'clock position in two. This line runs North–South. South lies halfway between the hour hand and the 12 o'clock position. North is directly opposite South.

position of the Sun

12 o'clock position points towards the Sun

North

In the southern hemisphere

In the southern hemisphere, point the 12 o'clock position at the Sun. North is halfway between this position and the hour hand. South lies in the opposite direction.

South

Bearing Safety in Mind

Follow a few simple rules to make sure your hiking trip is fun and safe.

- Always stay with your group and walk at the pace of the slowest person. Keep the walking pace even and steady, and rest regularly.

- Stay on marked footpaths. It's easy to get lost otherwise.

- Watch out for biting insects that may be brushed off onto your clothes. Tuck your trousers into your socks to protect your ankles from insect bites.

- Do not cross fallen logs that look unstable. Find another way around the obstacle.

- Eat and drink small amounts frequently.

Watch out for slippery rocks if you have to cross a stream.

Mountain Biking

If you're looking for a test of your skills, then mountain biking might be for you. It is similar to hiking in some ways – mountain bikers often follow marked trails on almost any terrain. However, the focus is on the physical challenge of pedalling a bike through the twists, turns and hills of an unpaved trail.

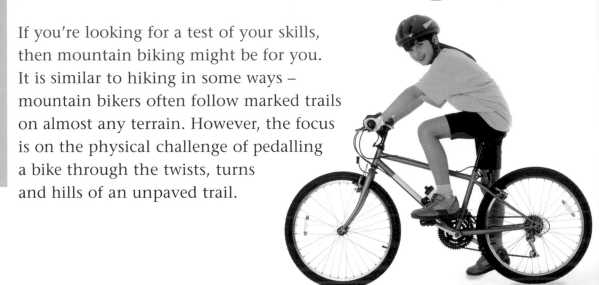

✔ Step One:
Getting Ready

Before setting out, talk to a mountain-biking instructor or visit a bike shop or website for advice about the clothes and equipment you will need. Mountain biking requires more specialized gear than hiking.

Equipment

Mountain bikes are designed to handle rugged terrain. They are more sturdy and have wider tyres than street and racing bikes. The handlebars are usually straight, unlike the curved handlebars of a racing bike.

A bike is a complicated piece of equipment. Learn about it before you set off on your trip. Find out how each part works. This information will be useful when making repairs.

Hints and Tips

Reflectors help make bikes visible to drivers if you're riding on the road. If your front or back reflector breaks or falls off, then replace it as soon as possible. Stick reflective strips to your bicycle helmet or clothing.

Parts of a Mountain Bike

saddle
handlebar
handlebar stem
brake lever
brake cable
water bottle
tyre
brake block
seat tube
front fork
toe clip
spoke
chain
valve

Clothing

Mountain bikers should wear stretchy, comfortable clothes that fit fairly close to the body and draw moisture away from the body. Loose clothing might become caught in the moving parts of the bike. Also wear bright clothing so you can be seen easily.

Padded cycling gloves help protect wrists by absorbing some of the jolts and bumps of mountain biking. They also help you to grip the handlebars, even in rain, and will protect hands from grazes if you fall. Wear closed shoes, not sandals, as exposed toes could get caught in the chain or spokes.

Wear stretchy, comfortable shorts.

Always wear a bicycle helmet. Check that it has been safety-tested. It should be lightweight with good ventilation.

Shoes with firm soles prevent your feet from getting sore.

A waterproof jacket will protect you from wind as well as rain.

Cycling gloves help you keep a firm grip on the handlebars.

Choosing a Route

Mountain biking is very different from cycling around town. Going up steep, rugged hills is tricky and tiring, and going downhill is dangerous. Cyclists need experience to control their speed and avoid obstacles. It's important to choose a trail that you and all the members of your group can handle.

Ask at a local bike shop or bike club which trails are suitable for beginners, and make sure the trails are open. Look for information about local trails in bookshops and libraries or on the internet. Major trails usually have trail maps available either at the site or on the internet. Some maps indicate the level of difficulty of a trail.

How to Read a Bike Trail Map

If you are planning a biking adventure, then you need to look for certain things on a map to plan the best route possible.

1 Study the map of your chosen area, and use the key to find out what each symbol means.

2 Are there trails that pass along rivers or through interesting terrain?

3 Use the contour lines and map scale to make sure your journey is not too long or too steep. Are there suitable rest stops?

4 Make sure your route avoids major roads. If you do need to cycle along a road, then be aware of the traffic rules.

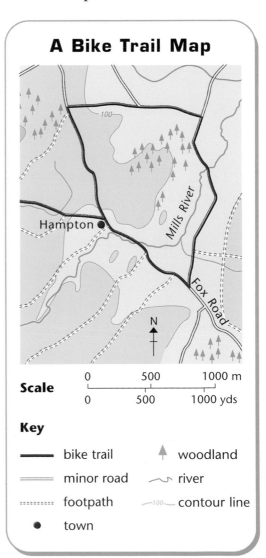

A Bike Trail Map

Hampton
Mills River
Fox Road
N

Scale	0	500	1000 m
	0	500	1000 yds

Key

——— bike trail   ♠ woodland

=== minor road   ～ river

:::::::::: footpath   —100— contour line

● town

Obstacles

Some trails are easier than others, but even the easiest trail is not completely flat. Rocks, logs, fallen branches and tree roots make a trail bumpy. Some obstacles can be ridden over. Others should not be attempted. Instead get off your bike and walk around them. Watch out for overhead obstacles as well. You may need to duck under branches or overhanging rock.

Mud

Cycling through mud can damage the environment by eroding, or wearing away, the ground. Carry your bike across patches of mud and other areas vulnerable to erosion. This also stops mud from getting into the moving parts of your bike and damaging them.

Water

If the water in a stream is very shallow (below the wheel hubs) and the stream bed is rocky or sandy, then riding across is usually acceptable. However, if the water reaches the hubs, then oil might leak into the water. Carry your bike across instead.
Do not attempt to cross deep water.

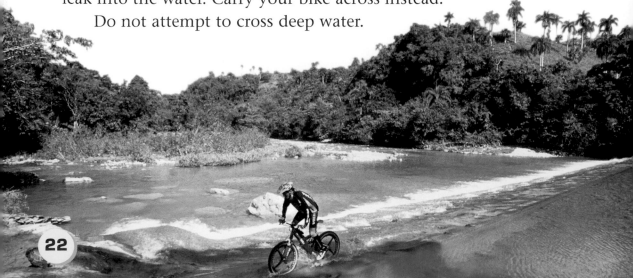

Trying Out the Basics

Mountain bikers must cycle over different terrains and obstacles. Knowing the correct techniques will make a ride easier and safer.

Riding Uphill

Stand on the pedals for gentle slopes, but always remain seated for steep hills. This weighs down the back wheel, and keeps it firmly on the ground.

1 Keep your weight in the centre of the bike, with your head forward and your arms bent. This will stop the front wheel lifting off the ground.

2 Grip the handlebars firmly and look straight ahead, not down at the trail.

Riding Downhill

Although downhill cycling is exciting, it is also dangerous. Do not go down a hill that seems too steep or bumpy.

1 Keep your weight back in the saddle and your arms straight.

2 Relax your knees, keep them bent and grip the handlebars firmly.

3 To freewheel, or coast, down a hill, keep the pedals level and control your speed by using the brakes when necessary.

Riding Around Bends

Sometimes you won't be able to see what's around a bend. There could be a fallen log or another rider. Be prepared to stop quickly.

Practise riding in a circle before you head for a trail. Remember to practise turning in both directions.

1 As you approach a bend in the trail, slow down.

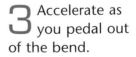

2 Lean into the bend with your hips as you turn the handlebars. If you feel unstable at any time, put one foot on the ground.

3 Accelerate as you pedal out of the bend.

Carrying Your Bike

When the ground is too bumpy or muddy to ride across, carry your bike past the obstacle.

1 Stand on the left-hand side of your bike to avoid getting grease from the chain on your clothes. Keep your back straight and bend from your knees.

2 Straighten your legs to lift the bike. Hold the handlebar stem with your left hand and the seat tube with your right. Lean the bike against you.

Making Emergency Stops

If you suddenly meet an obstacle, then you need to know how to stop your bike quickly and safely.

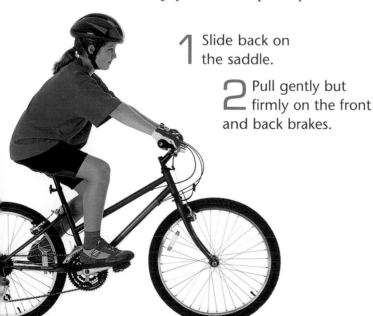

1 Slide back on the saddle.

2 Pull gently but firmly on the front and back brakes.

Hints and Tips

Pull equally on both brakes. If you pull too hard on the back brake, then the back wheel will lock and the bike will skid. If you pull too hard on the front brake, then the bike will tip forward.

Repairing a Hole in an Inner Tube

On rugged trails, flat tyres are a big problem. Each tyre has an inner tube filled with air. Rocks or thorns may pierce the tyre, then they might puncture the inner tube, allowing air to escape. Learn how to fix a flat tyre before setting out on a mountain bike. You'll need help removing the wheel and taking off the tyre to access the damaged inner tube.

A Puncture Repair Kit

repair kit containing small patches

larger, foil-wrapped patches

glue

sandpaper   wax crayon   chalk

1 Pump up the tube and listen and feel for escaping air. Or put the tube in water and look for bubbles. Draw a circle around the hole with the crayon.

2 Use sandpaper to roughen the area around the hole. This will help the repair patch stick to the tube.

3 Spread a small amount of glue around the hole. Let it dry for about five minutes.

4 Remove the backing from a patch and press it over the hole. Leave it for another five minutes.

5 If the repair kit includes chalk, then sprinkle some around the patch to soak up excess glue.

Bearing Safety in Mind

Mountain biking can be dangerous. Always stay alert, and slow down for any tricky situations. Bike trails are often crowded with riders going at different speeds and in different directions. Follow these rules for a fun and safe ride.

- Always check that you are allowed to ride on a trail, and don't leave the trail once you are on it.

- Give way to pedestrians. If the trail is narrow, then get off your bike and push it until there is more space to ride.

- Avoid narrow trails that pass too close to a river or lake.

- Let other riders know when you are going to pass. Call out to them or ring your bike's bell so the rider being passed knows to keep to the left.

- When another rider is coming towards you keep to the left as you pass each other.

- Approach a blind bend with caution. There might be someone on the other side.

Ride alongside the mountain bikers in your group only if it is safe to do so.

Canoeing

Canoeing is fun for everyone. While beginners take a leisurely trip on a calm river or lake, more experienced canoeists have the opportunity to travel down rougher waters. For all canoeists, there is the opportunity to explore the great outdoors from a different perspective.

There are three pieces of equipment required for canoeing: a life jacket or buoyancy aid, a paddle and, of course, a canoe. It is best to hire equipment as it is quite expensive.

Equipment

Canoes have one or two seats. Beginners usually start with a two-seater, with room between them for one or two passengers to sit on the floor of the canoe.

    The canoe shown here has two seats and one thwart – the bar that goes from one side of the canoe to the other. Paddlers sit on the seats, facing the bow (front) of the canoe. Passengers sit on the floor, also facing the bow. They often sit behind the thwart so they can hold on to it.

    Paddles come in many different lengths to suit people of different heights. Generally, the paddle should be almost as tall as the paddler. To choose the correct length, stand the paddle up next to your foot. The end of the paddle should come up to nose or eye level.

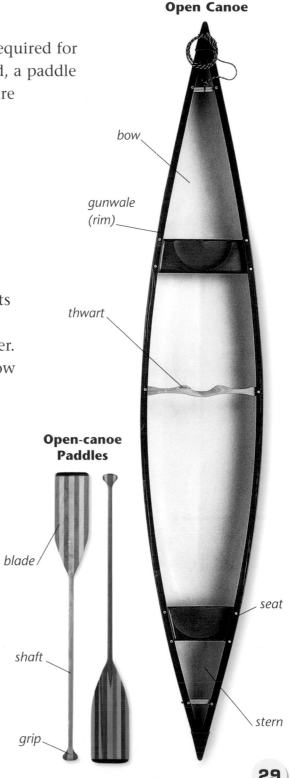

Open Canoe

bow

gunwale (rim)

thwart

seat

stern

Open-canoe Paddles

blade

shaft

grip

Clothing

Even the strongest swimmers need to wear a life jacket or buoyancy aid. This will help you float if you fall out of the canoe.

No special clothes are needed for canoeing. However, because the sport requires a lot of movement, loose-fitting clothes are best. Since you're bound to get wet, choose clothes that dry quickly. In cooler weather, wear warm, waterproof clothing or even a wetsuit. In sunny weather, wear suncream, sunglasses and a wide-brimmed hat.

Wear clothes that dry quickly.

A life jacket or buoyancy aid is a must for every canoeist.

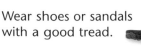

Loose-fitting clothing lets you move more easily.

Take a towel in a plastic bag.

Hints and Tips

Store valuables in a waterproof container that will float if it falls out of the canoe.

Wear shoes or sandals with a good tread.

Step Two:
Choosing a Route

Use a map to find good places to canoe. Look for rivers or lakes which are usually marked in blue on a map. Note their names, then use the internet or a guidebook to find out more about them.

Look for routes that do not have areas where the canoe has to be carried.

Lakes and ponds are good places to try canoeing. The water is usually calm, so a beginner can practise paddling techniques. Canoeing on a river is more difficult because there is a current, or water flow.

Lakes are great places for beginners to practise their canoeing skills.

How to Read a Map for Canoeing
Use maps or charts to plan your trips.

1 Look for recommended routes which are often indicated by a red line.

2 Then look for launch sites and note symbols that identify useful landmarks such as campsites. Check for marshland and other hazards. It is not safe to launch a canoe from marshland.

A Canoeing Map

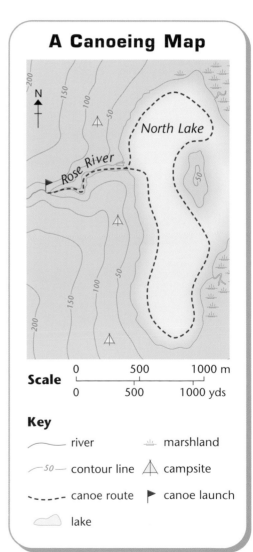

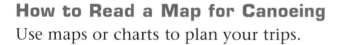

Scale

0	500	1000 m
0	500	1000 yds

Key

⌇⌇ river   ⅏ marshland

⌒50⌒ contour line   ⛺ campsite

- - - - - canoe route   ► canoe launch

⬭ lake

Gentle Currents

Expert canoeists have plenty of choices of places to travel. However, only some places are suitable for beginners. It is difficult to control a canoe if the water has a strong current. Some rivers also have dangerous obstacles such as large rocks.

Calm and slow-moving water is best for a beginner. However, watch out for obstacles even in calm water. Always make sure you wear a life jacket or buoyancy aid in case the canoe overturns.

Strong Currents

On a river with strong currents the canoeists need even more strength and skill. In the middle of a river the current is strong so the canoe will move downstream quickly. Near the banks of the river the current is less strong. By staying close to the banks, the canoeists can still move upstream without too much difficulty.

Rapids

Rapids are areas of fast-moving, shallow water and rocks. They are dangerous and should not be attempted by beginners. Most people who attempt rapids prefer to use a kayak. This is a special one-person canoe.

Step Three:

Trying Out the Basics

When two people paddle a canoe, the one who sits in the stern, or back, gets in first. A single canoeist should sit in the stern. New canoeists need a paddling partner. Steering and going faster are more difficult alone.

Before your first trip, learn the proper way to climb into a canoe. A canoeing instructor will help you practise these skills. Remember, you should always go canoeing with an adult who can swim.

Getting Into the Canoe

Place the paddle in the canoe before getting in to the canoe. Reverse the steps to get out of a canoe.

Hold the boat steady as your partner enters the canoe.

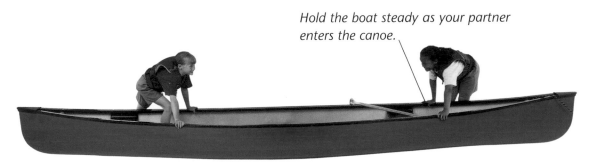

1 Facing the bow, or front, of the canoe, hold onto the nearest gunwale, or rim, and put one foot in the middle of the canoe.

2 Reach for the gunwale on the other side, keeping one hand on the near gunwale. Shift your weight onto the foot in the boat, bring in your other foot and sit down.

Hints and Tips

Usually, canoeists paddle only on their side of the canoe. Both paddlers should paddle evenly and at the same time to travel in a straight line.

How to Hold a Paddle

Before setting off, make sure you are holding
the paddle correctly.

1 Hold the paddle with both
hands. One hand should
be just above the blade.

2 Place the other
hand at the top of
the paddle on the grip.

Paddling Forward

Both the bow paddler and the stern paddler use the same basic
stroke. However, they generally stroke on opposite sides of the
canoe. If one person paddles on the left side while the other
paddles on the right, the canoe will keep going straight.
Use a paddle to push away from the shore.

1 Put the blade of the paddle
in the water.

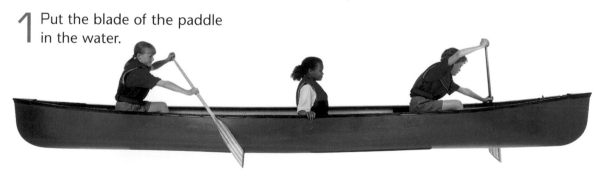

2 Draw the blade back by pulling
with the lower hand and pushing
with the top.

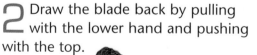

3 Take the paddle out of the water,
then dip it in again on the same side.

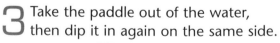

Turning the Canoe

To turn right gradually, both canoeists paddle on the left. To turn left gradually, both paddle on the right. To make a sharper turn, canoeists paddle on opposite sides.

1 Place the paddle in the water and sweep it in a wide arc. As the back paddler sweeps from stern (back) to bow (front), the front paddler does the opposite.

2 Repeat the stroke until the canoe has turned around.

Stopping the Canoe

To stop a canoe, reverse the direction of your strokes.

1 If you are moving forwards, then paddle backwards to stop.

2 If you are moving backwards, then paddle forwards to stop.

Step Four:
Bearing Safety in Mind

With a little practise, you will soon be exploring lakes or canoeing down rivers. Follow these safety tips to help avoid accidents.

- Carry a container to empty water that gets into the canoe.

- Always sit on the seats or in the middle of the canoe. Sitting on the sides will tip the canoe over.

- Always canoe with a partner so one can get help if the other is in danger.

- Stay low in the canoe and never stand up. Remember, canoes capsize easily.

- Never try to move from one boat to another in the water. Change boats only at a jetty or on the shore.

- Strong water currents move a canoe quickly. Paddle to shore if the current becomes too strong.

Always wear a life jacket or buoyancy aid when canoeing, even if the water is calm.

Safe and Sound

Each sport has its own rules and regulations. However, there are some suggestions that everyone should follow, no matter what activity they choose. The following information about health and first aid while outdoors is useful for anyone who participates in an outdoor sport.

Keeping Up Your Energy

To keep your energy levels up while excercising, take along some food. Fruit, sandwiches and cereal bars are good sources of nutrition and are easy to carry.

Water is very important. Dehydration is a serious loss of body fluids. It weakens the body, so make sure you have plenty of water. Always carry more than you think you will need in case a trip takes longer than expected. Do not drink water from lakes or rivers because it may be polluted.

Make sure you drink plenty of water.

Food and Drink for an Outdoor Trip

Pack a healthy meal that will give you plenty of energy.

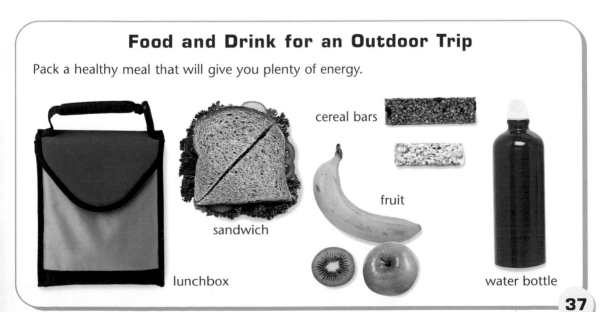

cereal bars

sandwich

fruit

lunchbox

water bottle

Protection Against the Sun

Even on cloudy days, the ultraviolet rays of the Sun can burn you. Wear a hat with a brim to protect yourself from the Sun, and use suncream to protect any exposed skin. Since the Sun is also harmful to your eyes, wear sunglasses, too.

suncream

Suncream and sunglasses are essential for outdoor activities, particularly during the summer months.

Protection Against Insect Bites

You'll find many different insects outside. Unfortunately, some of these insects bite or sting. Some even carry diseases. Wear an insect repellent to help prevent insect bites.

Wasps may sting if provoked.

Mosquito bites are very itchy.

insect repellent

First Aid

A first-aid kit and basic knowledge of how to use it can help you handle emergencies in the outdoors.

In any emergency, make sure the adult with you is aware of the situation. If the adult is injured, then find another adult to help you as quickly as possible. Try to stay calm. If the injury is minor, it can probably be treated with the items in the first-aid kit. Find a telephone and call for help if the person is bleeding a lot, has broken a bone or is unconscious or confused.

Remember that it is better to prevent accidents than respond to them.

Hints and Tips

Dial 999 in an emergency. Be ready to give details about the injury and the injured person as well as your telephone number and your location.

First-aid Kit

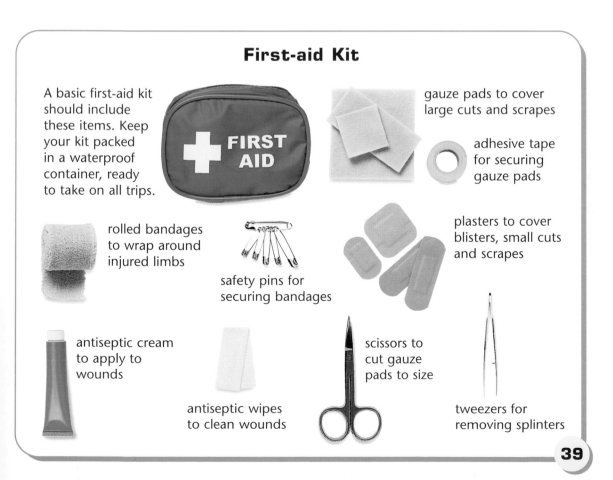

A basic first-aid kit should include these items. Keep your kit packed in a waterproof container, ready to take on all trips.

gauze pads to cover large cuts and scrapes

adhesive tape for securing gauze pads

rolled bandages to wrap around injured limbs

safety pins for securing bandages

plasters to cover blisters, small cuts and scrapes

antiseptic cream to apply to wounds

antiseptic wipes to clean wounds

scissors to cut gauze pads to size

tweezers for removing splinters

Index

Resources

For more information on hiking, mountain biking and canoeing, visit these websites:

- The Ramblers' Association: **www.ramblers.org.uk**
- British Cycling: **www.bcf.uk.com**
- British Canoe Union: **www.bcu.org.uk**